Considering Swinging

Ed and Dana Allen

Momentpoint Media

Considering Swinging
by Ed and Dana Allen

Copyright 2001 Ed Allen
ISBN 0-9710448-1-3

You are welcome to contact the authors via their website:

www.theswinginglife.com

Contents

Good Friends ... Great Fun

This is an invitation for you to consider swinging.

Swinging involves consensual and conjoint participation in sexual activities by a male–female couple with other people.

This definition might seem overly exact, but if the sexual activity isn't consensual (agreed to by everybody involved) and conjoint (enjoyed at the same time and general location) then it isn't really swinging. So, if you and your significant other agree to date other people on alternate Saturdays, you aren't swinging. Likewise, single people are sometimes invited to join in the fun, but it isn't swinging if there aren't couples involved. A single man or woman who claims to enjoy a "swinging lifestyle" is using the term in a different sense entirely. Finally, swinging is not a gay or lesbian lifestyle; it always involves at least one male-female couple, although either partner may be bi-sexual or bi-playful.

The vast majority of swingers, however, would right-fully proclaim that swinging consists of a lot more than the sexual interactions. Close friendships often develop among swingers. Perhaps this is because almost everyone finds that traditional social activities are less stressful and more fun when shared with folks who are comfortable with their sexuality and secure in their sexual relationships.

So the next time you notice several couples smiling and laughing and having a great time at a ball game, picnic, concert, or bar, you could well be correct if you imagine that they met each other at a swinging party.

Swingers generally understand that sexual guilt and shame are tools devised by politicians and priests to intimidate and subdue the populace. We resolutely believe in the right of all people to pursue happiness in their relationships, and we decry intrusion into our sexual lives by Big Brother and all his cohorts.

Mostly, though, we have fun! Fun with friends and fun with each other as we share our experiences in this exciting lifestyle.

Please consider joining us.

— Ed and Dana

What Is Swinging Like?

This is the most common question asked by those who are considering swinging. As with many of life's simple questions, there is no simple answer. Instead of trying to devise an all-inclusive yet precise response, we have chosen to include a number of "Swing Scenes" (interspersed throughout this booklet). Every incident, every place, and every person described in these Scenes are authentic, except not in the configurations and combinations presented. We have changed names and locations, but we have let our actual experiences dictate the settings, styles, and actions.

By reading these vignettes, you should gain a sense of the diversity of experiences that swinging encompasses. These experiences, as you might expect, are not always gratifying. Although we have written here only about the good times and the warm, loving people, we have had uncomfortable moments with a few cold, crass jerks (both male and female). But such moments really are few and far between. [Dealing with difficult times is one topic covered in our other book: *Together Sex*.]

Almost all the time, we're really enjoying ourselves, as these scenes attest.

Your experiences, of course, will be unique because nobody quite like you has ever been a swinger before. Nevertheless, if you are willing to learn from those who have gone before, your chances of finding real pleasure and true friendship are pretty darned good.

Swing Scene

Huddles & Cuddles

Should you be out strolling a certain street in Princeton on a Sunday afternoon, and wonder who lives in the elegant homes whose tops are barely visible above their stone walls, stop for a moment in the autumn sunshine, pick out one of the wrought-iron gates, and ponder what you might discover upon passing through the private garden and opening the oaken door.

If, just by chance, you choose the residence that we have in mind, you may be pleased or startled to witness a scene such as follows.

For all the tasteful conglomeration of modern furniture, oriental rugs, and paintings of every period that reflect the artistic backgrounds of George and Nancy, today their living room is reminiscent of an upscale tavern. Scotch and soda, beer and pretzels, cheese and crackers, are scattered in assorted silver and crystal dishes across the teakwood tables. A light haze of tobacco smoke by the French doors delineates the rays of the already setting sun. The television, squatting incongruously beneath an original Utrillo has momentarily gained dominance over the minds and hearts of the occupants of the room. Nothing takes precedence over football.

The captain's chair nearest to the TV holds Robert, a 37-year-old accountant with an unruly shock of hair that is totally and prematurely white. Perched on the ottoman next to him is his wife Pat, slender, small-boned, and pixyish. Ronald, in jeans and t-shirt, is sitting cross-legged on the floor by Robert's feet. Susan, her long brown hair drifting loosely around her shoulders, is Ron's date for the afternoon, but she is curled up on the yellow couch between Nancy and Carl.

A typical, friendly neighborhood gathering; except these folks have gathered from neighborhoods all around the city and they seem friendlier than most.

As the action on the field unfolds, the cheers and groans sound no different from a "normal" football-watching party. And as the interactions among the viewers play out, the sexual innuendos and flirtatious comments are about the same as you might expect from any mixed group of healthy adults. The responses those comments engender, though, might strike you as a bit more serious than normal. And, most puzzling, there is never any hint of disapproval from anyone's spouse, not even when celebratory kisses grow into passionate ones or knee squeezes become thigh rubs. You sense that everyone seems unusually relaxed with each other, although some couples have never met before.

When the game is over, George and Nancy's guests will celebrate or commiserate for a half-hour or so while fresh drinks are prepared, muscles are unkinked and bladders emptied. Someone will urge George to light the first logs of the season in the huge stone fireplace and slowly, subtly, the warm glow of the fire will merge with the warmth from the alcohol and people will start moving together.

Offers to lead a private tour of the house, "Have you seen his collection of Santa Clauses?" or, "Wait 'til you see the view from the third floor!", will propel several couples away from the social milieu and into one of the six bedrooms kept furnished for such purposes.

Giggles and moans, laughter and screams, will mingle with the sound of running water and bouncing bedsprings and drift down the stairs to the couples conversing before the fire. Throughout the evening the score or so party attendees will tread these stairs as various pairings and a few threesomes trade places amongst the paintings and sculpture.

It being a work-day eve, a few couples will leave by eight o'clock, gathering clothing, trading phone numbers and mumbling about the cost of baby-sitters. By nine, the six people remaining will gather in various stages of undress around the baby grand and spend a final, serene hour listening to Nancy play Bernstein and Webber.

Then a little washing up the glasses, a few kisses, a lot of hugs, and the party is over. ◄

The Top Ten Reasons Why You Really Ought To
Consider Swinging

Reason Number 10

Enjoyable Company. Swingers tend to be the kind of people that are exciting and fun to be with: honest, happy, vibrant, intelligent, knowledgeable, pleasant, attractive, and friendly. Enjoy being a swinger not only at dance parties, beach parties, pool parties, and just plain sex parties, but at picnics, ball games, art galleries, and all the places folks go together. Everything's more fun when shared with great people.

Reason Number 9

A remarkably healthy lifestyle. A social scene that discourages heavy alcohol consumption, generally prohibits drug use, and offers lots of opportunity for cardio-pulmonary exercise. Is that cool or what?

Reason Number 8

All dressed up with someplace to go. Now you have an opportunity to actually wear those daring dresses and leather lingerie you've seen in adult catalogs and sex shops. And, you won't get arrested, assaulted, or laughed at either. Even in more traditional party clothes, most women (and men too, but they often won't admit it) enjoy "getting all dolled up" and strutting their stuff now and then. Swinging will get you out and about more often than most any other hobby — and you'll look sharper while you're there.

Reason Number 7

Your fantasies fulfilled. Two men? Three women? All at once or in sequence? Same-gender? Large piles of anonymous flesh? Intimate moments with one stranger? With someone watching? With a crowd watching? While watching others? Maybe you just want a lot of good-looking people lusting after you as you dance. Whatever your fantasy, swinging can provide willing and discreet participants.

Reason Number 6

Improve your sexual techniques. You and your spouse might be very adept lovers, but you don't know it all. So how are you going to learn ... on the Internet?

Reason Number 5

Staying "swappable" is good for you. There's no motivation to stay with a diet or an exercise program that is as strong as the prospect of a swinging party. Sadly, many people stop trying to maintain their attractiveness once their marriage settles down. Well, shake it up!

Reason Number 4

Satisfy your appetite for variety. Big muscles or big boobs; shapely butts or pendulous pricks; blondes, blonds, red heads and bald heads; oral, anal and any 'ol way you can imagine; all are out there. You probably have a wonderful, loving, and sexy spouse, but why limit yourself to wonderful? You only get one visit to the smorgasbord of life — sample everything!

Reason Number 3

G ood **Friends**. Nothing outside one's family is more valuable than friendship. If you are fortunate, you have a few really good friends now. Stick around swinging for a while and you'll likely find several more. This intimate lifestyle is a wonderful way to increase your odds of meeting another couple that truly shares your interests and approach to life.

Reason Number 2

B etter **Friends**. It is a sad truth that friendships among couples are often broken (or at least cracked) by jealousy, envy, and similar sexual issues. The second-best reason to swing is the positive effects it can have on friendships. There is no reason to hide your desire for your buddy's wife when that desire is openly welcomed. There is no reason to be fearful of your husband having an affair behind your back when you can enjoy watching him right in front of you — and join in if you so desire. And, most importantly, everyone is just more relaxed and real once the natural and inevitable sexual tensions are vanquished from the relationship.

And the first top reason to consider swinging is ...

Reason Number 1

The couple that plays together … You may have heard talk of "non-monogamous" lifestyles. Well, this is just the opposite. If swinging meant simply "freely having sex with other people," it wouldn't need a special name. What makes swinging special is that couples do it together.

Few things draw marriage partners closer together than the social and sexual sharing of swinging.

Now, if you're thinking that you might not want to share your mate with someone else, consider that when you and your partner go to the movies together, you are not sharing him or her *with the movie*, rather, *the two of you share the experience* of watching the movie. And, shared experiences are the building blocks of strong relationships. Well, so it is with swinging. We are not suggesting that you share your mate with anyone. We *are* suggesting that you and your partner share with each other the joys of experiencing other people, both mentally and emotionally (which you do with your friends already) *and* physically.

Whether you party in the same bed or just tell each other stories afterward, you'll likely feel a tenderness towards, and an appreciation for, one another that no other experience can give you.

Of course, you have to work at it some, but if you do, and if your marriage is sound, swinging will make it better.

Dances With Sex

We remember dancing in many a bar and club....

D irectly across from the main doors are folding tables covered in white cloth with stacks of paper plates and carefully arranged rows of plastic wine glasses. Tonight's buffet is chicken wings, celery sticks, olives, and precisely cut cubes of yellow cheese with toothpicks. Oh, yeah, how could I forget the *piece de resistance*, the tiny bun-wrapped wieners with brown mustard. (Hmmm ... wieners wrapped in buns ... are they trying to tell me something?) Anyway, there's no danger of a visit by the editors of *Bon Appétit*. Which is just as well — they probably wouldn't understand the rest of the scene.

Now for the good stuff: A disc jockey playing music we can actually dance to. Room to maneuver on the expansive wooden floor of a hotel ballroom. ... Okay, it's really the tiled floor of a motel meeting room, but it's big enough and nice enough and there are actually a couple of chandeliers hanging above us. If there were crepe-paper streamers dangling over the doorways, I'd think I was dancing at my senior prom. This is much better, of course, as none of the guys are geeks and I don't have to pretend to be a virgin — that pretense being rather difficult for someone wearing a very short leather skirt and no panties.

Right now, Richard's left hand has lifted the front hem of that skirt and discovered the lack of garments beneath. Hallelujah!

11

Richard (at least I think his name is Richard) is one of the coolest guys at this bi-monthly soirée sponsored by "Lifestyle Socials." Being from way out of town, this is our first visit, so my husband and I have spent most of the first two hours trying to meet those folks that particularly attract us. Finally Jim, that's my husband, struck up a conversation in the men's room with Richard. (I wonder if they were peeing side-by-side. Jim didn't say anything about the size of Richard's penis. … Guess I'll have to find that out for myself.) Anyway, when they came back into the "ballroom" they acted like old fraternity buddies. So, Richard introduced us to his wife and some other couple whose names I don't remember, and then asked me to dance.

Okay, so I've only known this dude for a few minutes and he already has two fingers well into my pussy, does that make me a slut? Oh yeah?! Well, on Monday, I'll go back to being a middle manager in a major corporation — professional and stern as any staff member — tonight I'm Miss Hot Pants of the No-Tell Motel, and I love it! Gotta go now … or really … gotta … CUM … NOW !!!

"Why, thank you, Richard, that was an awfully nice dance."

I sure hope Jim is getting along okay with what's-her-name. ◄

As at many "off-premise" clubs, the clientele at "XC's Bar and Grill" sometimes push the envelope — "Well, it all depends on how you define 'having sex' doesn't it?"— and tonight is no exception. I look around the dimly lit room and see no mattresses in the shadows, no doors to tiny rooms, no vinyl harnesses suspended from the ceiling; only chairs and tables crammed with drink glasses and ashtrays. But on the dance floor itself, the action is hot and heavy. People aren't moving their feet much; there's hardly any room for that. Of course, this is the way they like it. Being packed shoulder to shoulder — "back to back and belly to belly" — while moving one's torso as sensuously as possible is the main attraction at XC's. (People certainly don't come for the conversation; you can hardly hear yourself yell over the music blasting throughout the place.)

But this is fine with me. Here, you can dance the way you always wanted to and not worry about what others might think, or about getting bounced out of the place. I enjoy rubbing up against firm tits and butts at least as much as I enjoy staring at them. And this is both a tactile and visual feast. Every where I look I see bodies bumping and rubbing to the beat. On my left, the most marvelous breasts are winning their battle to get free of a mostly unbuttoned shirt top. On my right, a couple have their hands down each other's pants, massaging butts while kissing passionately. And in front of me, my sexy wife has turned away from me, gyrating her ass back against my leg while some new gal bites playfully at her nipples.

And yes, cocks too. Making tents out of pants, poking out into inquiring hands, sometimes even into sucking lips.

That happened to me once, right here on this very floor. She was tall, slender, and gorgeous. I never thought I could do it so publicly, but she had the finest, wettest action I ever felt. I came and came and she didn't let a drop touch the floor — as those around us stared with envy. Later I discovered that her personality was just as fine as her technique and I looked forward to playing together in more comfortable surroundings. But, she decided to have a child, dropped out of the scene, and I haven't seen her since.

I, of course, was devastated. When I told my sad tale to other friends, however, they just didn't seem to feel very sorry for me. Can't figure why. ◄

.

OK, so it sounds like fun, *But What About ...?*

INHIBITIONS

You probably don't have a lot of inhibitions, or you wouldn't be reading this. On the other hand, few non-swingers have much experience with group sex. Don't let this deter you. Almost all swinging situations are free of pressure and expectations. You should be allowed to adjust to new situations and become involved at your own pace. If you are ever in a place where you feel uncomfortable because you are being pushed to do something — leave. You might return later, after you've gained familiarity with the scene, or you might learn later that you didn't belong there in the first place.

A little bit of apprehension, though, is to be expected. Even veteran swingers will often get a few butterflies in the tummy before going to a new club or attending a party with new people. This sort of anticipatory response is actually positive. When the day comes that you can remain blasé throughout your swinging activities, it's probably time to find some other hobby.

For optimum swinging fun follow these two maxims:

▸ If you're not sure, go ahead and try.
▸ If it hurts, stop.

And, of course, observing the Golden Rule isn't such a bad idea either.

DISEASE

Swinging is not risk-free. You could have an automobile accident on your way to a party, or on your way back home. You could get hit by lightening as you walk to the front door. You could slip on a spilled drink and bust your butt. You could be scalded in the shower. The party house could burn down with you in it. You could be exposed to second-hand smoke, get bit by the host's dachshund, or catch a disease by shaking hands with someone. And yes, you could catch a disease via sexual contact.

Knowing all this is not going to stop you from driving, walking, drinking, showering, or interacting socially. Should it stop you from outside sexual contacts?

We cannot eliminate risk in life, nor can we live forever. All we can do is work to minimize unacceptable levels of risk. Swingers have either decided that the risk of sexually-transmitted disease is so slight as to be acceptable, or they have adopted ways of reducing that risk to an acceptable level. Those in the first group point out that the incidence of disease among swingers is extremely low, and the incidence of deadly infection seems to be nonexistent. Approaches taken by the second group may include: having sexual encounters only with other couples who have been together a long time; using condoms; limiting most interactions to manual, or oral stimulation; or sticking mainly to watching and being watched.

Whatever you decide, don't be surprised if you change your minds several times.

MORALITY

"Thou shalt not commit adultery."

What, exactly, does this commandment mean?

"Adultery," according to our dictionary, means "sexual intercourse between a married person and one other than the lawful spouse." But leaders of the tribe of Semitic nomads who first wrote down this admonishment didn't have the same dictionary. What they meant by adultery must be inferred from other parts of their writings.

A careful reading of what we call "The Old Testament" clearly shows that the original (authentic) version of "Thou shalt not commit adultery," when translated into modern terms, should read: "Do not have sex with any of the wives of your tribesmen."

Men, back in those "good ol' days," could have all of the wives they wished and could afford. Those wives, of course, were duty bound to have sex with their husband and him alone. Unmarried women were fair game to all men. And soldiers were often encouraged by their leaders and their priests to rape the wives of neighboring tribesmen. So the ban against adultery was really an intra-tribal property-protection act; wives were chattel and not allowed to enjoy physical relations with anyone but their master. Their masters could have whomever they wanted.

If you can accept this as a reasonable approach to the marriage relationship, then please don't swing.

FEAR OF LOSS

You have a great deal invested in your relationship with your primary partner. You naturally want to minimize your risk of losing that investment. That's a tough job in this world.

Divorce rates today remain near their all-time highs — there's only a 50-50 chance that a new marriage will succeed. And that success is measured by longevity, not happiness. Therefore, many of these technically "successful" marriages will suffer from affairs, deception, and cheating. The hard truth is that our society's idea of marriage doesn't really work ... and never did.

One of the main problems is that, despite religious and political proclamations to the contrary, human beings are not naturally monogamous. The whole "cleave only to each other 'till death do us part" thing is a fiction invented by medieval troubadours — people have rarely acted that way and never actually felt that way.

Most of us do want a secure, permanent relationship with a loving partner, but we cannot easily repress the natural urge to enjoy variety in our sexual pursuits. Nor should we — to make sex the one exclusive aspect of a relationship is to sow seeds of destruction in that relationship.

An increasing number of men and women are choosing instead to use their natural sexual inclinations to reinforce the bonds of their relationship.

The essence of swinging is togetherness. Swinging is inclusive honesty, not divisive lying; communication, not concealment. Swingers don't cheat on each other, they share with each other. And shared good times are relationship builders, not relationship destroyers.

Of course, divorce is not entirely unknown in the swinging world — there are stresses on a marriage other than sexual ones. But doing things the traditional way is even riskier. So, why not eliminate one of the biggest threats to your marriage?

As long as you and your mate have a loving relationship to begin with, do this together, and communicate completely, you'll find your relationship just gets stronger with every swinging encounter.

| Swing Scene | # Drive-By Viewing |

It's a good thing I had driven motorhomes before. They're huge and ungainly and steering requires a different touch than cars or even my big van. I felt complimented when Derek asked if I wanted to take over for awhile — he didn't trust just anybody with such responsibility. That is, I felt complimented until I realized that Derek had plans other than keeping me entertained while I drove. I mean, I enjoyed piloting the gigantic Pace Arrow down the four-lane, but it was obvious that the other five friendly folk were going to have an incomparably better time becoming even more friendly in the back.

My wife and I, Derek and Joanne, and three other couples were returning to the city after a fine weekend sharing a beach house — six of us in the motorhome with the other four following in Wayne's black Chevy van. So far, the trip had been uneventful, except for the moment when the three representatives of the gentler gender in the motorhome had dropped their shorts, stood rather precariously on the rear couch, and — after Derek had called Wayne on the CB and directed his attention to the Pace Arrow's rear window — had yanked open the curtains and given a triple moon to Wayne and whoever else was behind us on the highway. (Note, this procedure is not endorsed by the National Highway Safety Council ... after all, the women were not wearing their seatbelts.)

As I drove through the darkening summer evening, Derek set up his 8-millimeter projector (this was before the advent of video), threaded in a "dirty" movie, and hung a white sheet across the aisle. Like I said before, it was a good thing I was comfortable driving that land yacht or I might have been more than a bit distracted by the scene in my rearview mirror. (There is absolutely no truth to the slanderous rumor that "Miles almost drove off the road" every time a particularly juicy scene developed.)

I was finding the whole spectacle pretty humorous, although I did feel a little left out. Then, Wayne called from the van behind to report the erratic behavior of several tractor-trailers as they passed us in the opposite lanes. We had closed the curtains in the back, but we hadn't thought that oncoming truckers sitting high in their rigs would be treated to a most unusual road show through the large windshield of the Pace Arrow.

So we gave in to sensibility and shut down the traveling theater, giving thanks that police cars aren't as high as 18-wheelers. Actually, I was thankful for more than that — when everyone moved back up front, Joanne crawled between my knees and sucked my cock for awhile. Now *that* *was* distracting ... but I had my seatbelt on. ◄

Key Concepts and Terms

To communicate comfortably within the swinging scene, here are the main words and phrases you should understand plus a few to avoid.

For a more complete list (including the arcane, bizarre, and witty) see www.theswinginglife.com or the appendices of *Together Sex*.

APPROACHES

In its broadest sense, the term OPEN MARRIAGE signifies cooperation between marriage partners without dependence, flexible roles, individual sanctity and growth, privacy, equality, trust, etc. Interpreted thusly, most swingers have open marriages. More narrowly, the term denotes an agreement between husband and wife to permit sexual activities independent of one another (*i.e.* to date others). Such activity is not swinging, and many would say it is the antithesis of swinging.

And why, you might ask, is that? Well, because the term SWINGING describes activities involving consensual and conjoint participation in sexual interactions by a male-female couple with other couples. So, while having sex outside of an open marriage might be consensual (agreed to by everyone involved), it is not conjoint (enjoyed together).

Those who like to analyze social phenomena sometimes use the term RECREATIONAL SWINGING to indicate an emphasis on the playfulness of social/sexual interactions, as opposed to UTOPIAN or GROWTH SWINGING, terms that indicate an emphasis on deep commitments, shared responsibilities, and long-term relationships. The currently fashionable term for multilateral relationships involving a broader commitment than normally associated with recreational sex is POLYAMORY (many loves). In reality, the boundaries between these classifications are rather indistinct and porous. Most swingers, in our experience, are interested in enduring friendships. On the other hand, few folks try to set up long-term housekeeping with other couples, and *very* few succeed for long.

Because it implies a male-dominated bartering of wives as possessions, the term "wife-swapping" is no longer used as a synonym for swinging. (Actually, it was never an accurate appellation anyway; as any veteran swinger will tell you, it's the women who usually run the swinging show.) "Spouse swapping" or "mate swapping" likewise have overtones of ownership and are generally shunned

PEOPLE

People who have been swingers for only a short while are called BABY SWINGERS, as opposed to VETERANS. If at a swinging social for the first time, they are NEWBIES. Those who seem attracted but don't participate are WANNABES.

BISEXUAL (or simply BI) can mean that a person is attracted to males and females pretty much equally. Such a non-preference, however, is rare. Usually, when someone says they are bisexual, they mean that they are attracted to their own gender, but not as much as to their opposite gender (could be less, could be more). Synonyms for bisexual include VERSATILE, AMBI-SEXUAL, and AC/DC, although the •latter is going out of favor. The term BI-CURIOUS means just what is sounds like, *i.e.* inexperienced but interested to know what same-sex interactions would be like. Then there is BI-PLAYFUL, which means someone who feels no attraction to the same gender, but who has no hang-ups that preclude a bit of friendly fooling around when the situation seems to call for it.

If people are called HARD CORE they are thought of as: (a) exercising little or no selectivity in choosing sex partners, and/or (b) participating in swinging with an almost religious fervor, as often as circumstances allow, and/or (c) wanting no more emotional or mental involvement than is absolutely necessary to complete the sexual encounter. We've never known anyone to apply this term to themselves.

A person who prefers oral-genital contact to genital-genital contact might be called a HEAD JOCKEY. Sometimes a man is motivated to earn this appellation because he has an exceptionally small penis or exceptional difficulty attaining an erection. A woman who suffers discomfort from vaginal penetration could do likewise. [We always appreciate such creative responses to life's little difficulties.]

A small but significant percentage of swingers enjoy some form of BDSM (Bondage, Discipline, Sadism, Masochism) and may be either DOMINANT or SUBMISSIVE.

A TICKET is a non-swinging person (usually female) brought to a couples-only swinging activity solely to enable another person (male) to gain entrance. This practice is severely frowned upon.

A PRIMARY BOND is a dyadic relationship (such as husband to wife) that takes precedence over other relationships. Your PRIMARY PARTNER is the one who came to the party with you.

GATHERING PLACES

Although you never hear about it in the media, the vast majority of swinging takes place in private homes, often just two couples getting together for the evening, but private parties of three or more couples are also prevalent. Swinging is very much a network activity. People tend to introduce new friends to old friends and the circles keep expanding. But, there are nodes in the network — places where swingers congregate to socialize in larger and more public settings.

Almost any of these gathering places might be termed a CLUB. (This can also refer to an organization of swingers, rather than a place.) Virtually all clubs have a bar of some sort and a dance floor; beyond these, the amenities vary over a wide range. The most critical distinction among clubs is whether they are on-premise or off-premise.

As you might assume, an ON-PREMISE club is one that provides facilities (beds, spas, etc.) for sexual activity in addition to, and usually separated from, a general meeting/dancing/dining area. An on-premise club can be located in commercial space such as a converted nightclub or a suite in an industrial park, or it might be in a PARTY HOUSE that is open only occasionally and is someone's private home the rest of the time.

In most locales, on-premise clubs try to maintain a low profile and are careful to screen new members, lest the local busybodies get wind of them and try to shut them down. There could be an on-premise club near where you live, but unless it advertises on the Internet or you know someone who is a member you are unlikely to discover it. In the few locales where swinging is more tolerated, on-premise clubs compete openly with one another and are much less restrictive in their membership policies. Such clubs tend to draw larger crowds (which can be good) and more folks that are "just looking" (which can be not-so-good).

OFF-PREMISE clubs are of two types, bars and socials. A BAR is a restaurant or cocktail lounge that is open on one or more nights a week exclusively for swingers. Some bars allow, or even encourage, nudity or partial nudity and tolerate varying degrees of sexual interaction among the revelers. (The extent of such tolerance depends on local laws and the current level of interest taken by the police and the alcohol control boards.) The term SOCIAL denotes a function rather than a particular place. Typically, socials are held in hotel ballrooms where activities are limited to publicly acceptable behaviors such as eating, drinking, dancing, and conversing. (Sometimes the dancers do get *real* close.) The hotel's rooms are available, of course, and the social's sponsor might reserve a section of rooms for members to utilize as they desire.

PRACTICES

Swinging can be enjoyed in two basic ways. OPEN SWINGING involves sexual activity among two or more people that is open to the view and often the participation of others (such as the primary partners or other party attendees). This is sometimes referred to as SAME-ROOM swinging. CLOSED SWINGING is sexual interaction between two people that takes place in a more or less private place such as a separate room or curtained-off area of a club. Both forms are popular, but open swinging seems more prevalent, probably because couples have a greater sense of sharing and togetherness when they can see and touch one another.

Recently, the term SOFT SWINGING is being used by some to mean enjoying various sexual interactions (watching, fondling, licking, etc.) without exchanging partners for actual penetration. As at teenage make-out parties, such resolutions not to "go all the way" are often short-lived. Nevertheless, many couples find soft activities a good way to ease into swinging.

Originally, "soft swinging" was used as an antonym of "hard-core," to indicate that people were interested in friendships and not "just sex." The wise swinger will ask for more specifics whenever this preference is announced.

Specific types of sexual activities are sometimes referred to as CULTURES or ARTS. These are classified by prefixing the name of a country or society that is supposedly known for such inclinations. Cultures include:

"English" (spanking),

"French" (oral),

"German" (discipline),

"Greek" (anal), and

"Swedish" (manual).

While "bisexual" [see page 23] refers to a psychological orientation, SAME-SEX is only a description of an activity. It implies nothing about the level of desire (if any) that one participant feels for another.

Other than the standard meaning, the term PARTY is often used as a euphemism for sexual interaction, as in "Let's party." or "Did you ever party with them?"

CONTACTING

Following are a few terms you should understand when perusing ads on the Internet, in magazines, or in newspaper classifieds. (For thorough guidance on writing and placing an effective ad, see chapter 3 of *Together Sex*.)

DISCREET — Not likely to do or say anything that might reveal a swinger's identity.

DISCRETION — An indication of the need for caution so that children or others who may open mail or answer the telephone will not be offended or made aware of the swinging activity.

GENEROUS — A person willing directly or indirectly to pay money for whatever sexual material or interaction is offered. WEALTHY means the same.

MIXED — A biracial partnership.

MODERN MARRIEDS — Sometimes used when advertising in a newspaper or magazine that is not sexually oriented. Indicates a married couple who enjoy some form of sexual interaction with others.

SAFE — Used to describe a person who is sterile. Usually a man who has had a vasectomy.

Terms to Avoid

Several terms commonly used (particularly in personal ads) fail to convey any useful information and can only lead the reader to infer a lack of social skills on the writer's part.

The prime example of these Buzz Words is "ATTRACTIVE." It's pretty safe to assume that virtually all advertisers think of themselves as attractive, so the term is not going to distinguish you in any positive way. Also, using the term implies that you think other swingers are not as attractive as you, which suggests either vanity or ignorance. Better to describe your attributes (mental, emotional, and physical) more specifically and let readers decide for themselves if they might be attracted to you.

Other terms to avoid are

BARBIE & KEN — A "sour-grapes" reference used by the overweight or unattractive to disparage the expectation of pleasing proportions. As in: "I trust you're not looking for Barbie and Ken."

CLEAN — A buzz word meaning almost nothing except that the users believe themselves to be free of sexually transmitted diseases.

HEAVIES — A buzz word meaning anyone the user doesn't like who weighs more than the user weighs.

OLD — A buzz word meaning anyone the user doesn't like who was born before the user.

PROFESSIONAL — A buzz word used to suggest that the user is better educated than the average advertiser.

SAFE SEX — A misnomer (because nothing in life is "safe") often meant to indicate an insistence on the use of condoms during intercourse, but that could mean a wide variety of restrictions and/or artifacts. Better to be specific.

S.A.S.E. (Self-Addressed Stamped Envelope) — 1. A way to imply popularity. 2. An indication of a monetary motivation for placing the advertisement.

SELECTIVE — A buzz word denoting an assumed characteristic that is used as an excuse when the user doesn't like someone. Also, an ego support for those who are unsure of themselves.

SLENDER — A buzz word meaning anyone who weighs the same or less than the user weighs.

SQUARE — A buzz word indicating a person who is not as liberal as the user.

STRAIGHT — A word with entirely too many meanings. 1. Not bisexual, bi-curious, bi-playful, or homosexual. 2. A non-swinger. 3. Not sadistic, masochistic, or whatever else the user believes is perverted. 4. A person who does not use drugs, other than alcohol. 5. Square.

WAY-OUT — A buzz word meaning anyone who indulges in acts that the user doesn't care for. As in "We're not interested in anything way out." (Same goes for BIZARRE, PERVERTED, UNNATURAL, WEIRD, etc.) Better to be precise ... best to keep your options open.

Swing Scene

Sun, Set, Party

One advantage to playing tennis in the nude is that you don't sweat-up your clothes. This plus may be somewhat counterbalanced by the lack of a place to put your extra tennis balls, but overall I still prefer the uniform assigned by the big-Coach-in-the-sky.

Christie and I first attended a nudist club (or "camp" or "resort" or whatever you want to call them) about six years ago and discovered that it took us no more than five seconds to get comfortable with our nakedness. Approximately one-half hour later we felt we were accustomed to everyone else being nude. As we left that first evening we had convinced ourselves that it really wasn't a sexual stimulation - just like all the magazines said. After a week or so we had adjusted to seeing unbelievably fat and astoundingly old bodies without even slightly grimacing. In about a month we started feeling strange when we had our clothes *on*.

Once we really felt comfortably at-home at a nudist club we began to appreciate the sexual aspects that we had previously not noticed — or ignored. And, I must admit, I have yet to be able to play tennis, or ping-pong, or volleyball, or even chess with a nude woman and maintain total concentration on the game.

Anyway, as the California sun cooked the concrete beneath my aching feet, I was forced to admit that this lithe girl with her hair pinned back over her ears had beaten me fair and square. "Hey," I yelled across the sagging net, "let's quit all this nonsense and get a drink." I wasn't dying of thirst but I had to stop the carnage somehow. It's not that I consider myself a great athlete, but Sally really wasn't either, and I was getting embarrassed.

The sight of her glistening breasts bobbing around as she trotted toward me got my mind off the game quickly. Sally was five foot two, eyes of grayish green, with a subdued yet perpetual smile. She looked up and winked as my arm went around her shoulder and we headed toward the rooms so quaintly called "cabins" in the club's brochure.

None of the other friends we had come up with were visible among the assortment of sun lovers and "cottontails" crashing around the volleyball court. Sally's husband, Ned, had become an enthusiastic devotee of sitting in the whirlpool baths during the afternoon. Christie stayed in or near the swimming pool whenever possible. The other four couples who had formed our caravan from Santa Maria were most likely sharing the pool or playing ping-pong on the adjoining terrace.

Sally and I, who had known each other for six months now, enjoyed a rare feeling of alone-togetherness as we entered the tiny bedroom. Looking back, I am surprised at how clearly I remember the scene. Her tossing her racquet onto a chair and sitting easily on the bed's edge, raising one knee up and untying a white sneaker. A simple, everyday action, yet intimate and enticing.

I moved in front of her and lifted her chin to see her eyes. "Well ... hello," she whispered. Her hands reached out to cup my balls and lightly touch my stirring cock. Then her head bent to me and with an excruciatingly tender grasp her lips moved to hold me.

For a long time we both tasted the slippery saltiness of each other's warm skin. It must have been almost an hour later that we finally oozed apart and lay back panting on the bedspread. Even then, we might have remained unaware of our audience if they had refrained from cheering and clapping and tapping on the window. Someone opened the door and six friendly voyeurs filled the room with sun-reddened flesh and laughter.

"I'm glad you bastards enjoyed the show," I growled, "but the view was better from here." ◄

Customary Rules and Etiquette

Every club has its own standards and every host their own ways of doing things, but you won't go wrong if you follow these four guidelines at any swinging event — and if you don't, you'll probably wish you had.

Never pressure.

"No means NO" is the first rule stated in just about every book, brochure, and web site concerning swinging. And this is good because coercion definitely has no place in free, healthy, and playful sexual interactions.

Should someone rebuff your advances or resist your suggestions, you must immediately and graciously cease your efforts. Saying "Come on, I know you'll like it." or even "Why not?" is rude and prohibited behavior. This rule, by the way, applies to both genders. Some women have a difficult time accepting that every man doesn't lust after them.

Any socially competent person will realize, however, that "No means no" is an over-simplification.. "No" *can* mean other things, such as "Not without begging" or even "Please push me because I don't want to take responsibility for doing this." Nevertheless, the wise person never assumes such meaning without firm corroborating evidence.

And then there is the "no" that really means "not now." We have had lots of great sexy times with people who weren't enthusiastic when we first met — either because they were tired, distracted, satiated, or were in pursuit of someone else. So, while you should never push, it is often fruitful to try again another time.

No drugs.

If there is one case where "no" always means "absolutely not!" it is the universal prohibition of illegal drugs at swinger's clubs. This is not only a safety issue — things get wild enough without having someone freak out in the hot tub — it's a basic survival issue. Charges of sexual impropriety can be fought in court, but a drug bust will shutdown a club every time.

At private parties, some drugs *might* be tolerated, but always get permission from your host before bringing anything illegal into their home.

Take care of each other.

Swinging is a couple's endeavor. Even if you end up in separate rooms, you are responsible for your partner. Should he or she become drunk, angry, sick, lonely, or just plain irritable, it is up to you to unobtrusively remedy the situation or take him or her home. Never abdicate this responsibility to your host or to whomever your partner happens to be with when the problem arises.

Be nice.

The fact that the attendees openly enjoy sex makes them *more* human not less, so always act with the same courtesy, sensitivity, compassion, and forbearance that you would employ at a regular social gathering. The only way you might act differently is not to drink as much. Generally, when the rule of civility is violated, too much alcohol is a contributing factor.

Swing Scene

Pastoral Grouping

Being a Saint Bernard, Copernicus often carries friendliness to the point of obnoxiousness, but on that beautiful spring day I couldn't have been happier to see him bounding down the gravel drive to meet our car. Driving through the Poconos, the fertile May air washing over us in our topless Mustang, was invigorating. Blossoms and fresh greenery and warm sunlight had made us forget the stifling city, but offered little relief to our tired butts and cramped legs. If Copernicus had been a gorilla we would still have been glad to arrive. Licking our hands, he loudly, and needlessly, announced our arrival to his folks.

It had been a long time since we had seen our host and hostess. But friends like these never seem to change. Wyatt and Sharon are a study in contrasts. Both of them were born and raised in these mountains, yet they travel more than almost anyone else we know. They seem equally at ease explaining the habits of the native possums and discussing the activities of a movie star at a New Orleans' party during Mardi Gras. This smooth meshing of country and cosmopolitan is reflected throughout their large Victorian farm house. Even the doorway from which Wyatt appears as we stretch our limbs gives a hint of the lifestyle lived here. From the road, it appears to be a sign informing visitors of the historic significance of the frame home; however, the bronze plate actually proclaims, "Si Non Ocillas, Noli Tintinnare."

Despite our proclivity to ocillas, we have never rung that doorbell. I am certain Wyatt and Sharon would be insulted if we did. Good and gracious people such as these make wherever they are a home to their friends, and who rings the doorbell at home?

Once we had settled in, had a couple of cold beers and a country ham sandwich, Sharon convinced us to put on our hiking shoes and check out the view from the top of the mountain.

For close to three hours we half followed a path and half followed Copernicus around the mountainside, not quite attaining the top before we had to turn back. When we reached the house again, carrying assorted bouquets of wild flowers and spring ferns, the sun was hanging orange on the horizon.

Wyatt and Sharon made a few last minute dinner preparations while I fixed a pitcher of Bloody Marys. The mountain evening was turning chill so Matt lit a fire and we all plopped down in the enormous living room to talk and wait for the other guests to arrive. Seven other couples were expected. Each invited by one of Sharon's long, warm letters similar to the ones we receive two or three times a year.

It had been four years since we met this beautiful couple. Perhaps we have seen each other on a dozen occasions since. Our relationship is a great combination of relaxed friendship and exciting novelty. The time that passes between our visits is short enough to retain a comfortable familiarity yet long enough to provoke a pleasant expectancy when we come together again.

Before our glasses were half empty we heard the familiar roar of a diesel engine out front. "Well, the old wagon made it again," Wyatt exclaimed as we all jumped up and headed out to see what new toys Jimmie and Joni had added to their converted Greyhound bus.

"One of these days you guys are going to buy a muffler for that contraption," Wyatt shouted in an affected hillbilly drawl.

"Couldn't take the extra weight," answered Joni as she descended the steps with her overnight bag. "Don't want us stuck in one of your God-forsaken hollows do you?"

"Who cares when you are in this bus, long as you don't run out of gas for the refrigerator."

That soft raspy voice could only have belonged to one man. "Paul!" I shouted. "Oh it's good to see you! Wyatt didn't say you were coming."

"Well somebody had to keep Joni company while Jimmie piloted this craft," Paul said with a wink. "You know how she hates to watch TV alone."

Paul's wife, Sandra, gave her husband a not-so-gentle kick in the pants as she descended the steps behind him. "The only show I saw was a tired old re-run," she taunted. "Godzilla meets Wonder Woman."

Jimmie appeared next and invited us in to see the mirrors he had just installed in the bus' master bedroom, but the lights of another car coming up the driveway diverted our attention.

By nine o'clock, everyone had arrived and been assigned a sleeping space. By eleven, about half the party had
moved into one bedroom or another. Matt, Sharon, Paul
and I were into talking before the fire and smoking some of
the fine dried leaves that Wyatt so carefully cultivated in his
backyard. Each leaf had been separately picked and dried
with tender loving care and it seemed like too good an opportunity to miss.

Before long we had taken off our clothes and made a
giggling sandwich of our bodies beside the hearth. For what
seemed like hours we cuddled there sensing the others moving in and out of the room while Paul's low voice talked
about the crazy things that happened at the ski lodge he and
Sandra operate.

Then the drive and the hike and the herbs caught-up
with me and I slept. The fire gave out completely about
three o'clock and I awoke to find Matt unrolling a sleeping
bag beside me. Gratefully, I crawled into its warmth and
watched as he unrolled another bag and laid it over the en-
twined figures of Sharon and Paul. When Matt got into the
bag with me we cuddled together and I could feel him getting hard against my thigh. Still semi-floating, I reached
down and guided him into me.

The different surroundings gave a different yet pleasing rhythm to our movements and we both came together
quickly. I was almost asleep once more before he slid out
and settled beside me.

* * *

No matter how carefully you make out your guest list, it never fails to happen. Some obnoxiously cheery morning person wakes up with the birds and goes tramping about the house making a general nuisance of himself. If Wyatt had covered the floor with mattresses instead of carpeting I might have been able to ignore Phil's bustling and gotten back to sleep, but it was no use.

Sharon was awake beside me so we got up together and headed for the kitchen. (Well, after we headed for the bathroom.) In a few minutes Wyatt came down and decided it was such a beautiful morning that he would bless the world with a batch of his "famous" blueberry pancakes.

Within a half an hour the entire household was awake and most of them, Copernicus included, were in the sunny kitchen. Wyatt had every task organized. Arlena was squeezing fresh orange juice. Paul was pouring out coffee. Phil was assigned to fry several pounds of bacon and ham. Sharon was stacking plates, napkins, and silverware on the massive table. Those who had no specific duties sat around and kibitzed.

Breakfast turned out to be a great success, as did the entire stay. I even managed to spend a blessedly undisturbed hour in the den reading the Sunday paper. ◀

Answers to Questions
Commonly Asked About Swinging

How can a couple know if they are likely to be successful swingers?

Swinging involves being sexually playful as a couple with other couples. Almost by definition then, successful swingers will have four personal traits: 1. They really like sex. 2. They have a playful attitude toward life in general and sex in particular. 3. They enjoy doing things together with their spouses/partners. 4. They like to socialize with other people.

Now, if you didn't like sex or socializing, you most likely wouldn't have read this far, so the key concerns here are playfulness and togetherness.

Let's consider togetherness first. A couple is not likely to find happiness in swinging if that is the only activity they do as a couple. If she spends her free time with her female friends while his idea of going out is hanging with the guys, or if they do not converse easily and share their most intimate thoughts and desires — in short, if they are not each other's best (or, at least, very good) friends, then swinging could prove to be a real challenge to their relationship. Of course, swinging just might be the catalyst needed to bring them closer, but the better approach is to build a close partnership first, and then expand it into the swinging world.

For an in-depth treatment of playfulness, we must refer you to our other book, *Together Sex*. Here,

41

we only have space to say that being playful involves pursuing activities for the pleasure involved therein, rather than to accomplish some outside goal. The playful couple realizes that joy, laughter, orgasms, and other sensory delights are their own rewards. Playing at sex requires no more justification than building sand castles, writing poems, or dancing.

Sexual playfulness often involves activities such as giving each other sensual massages, taking baths together, masturbating in front of each other, sharing x-rated videos and books, doing private things in public, testing various toys, experimenting with restraint, trying new positions, and exploring every bodily orifice. If your relationship has been open to such things in the past, then you'll probably have an easy transition into swinging. If it hasn't, then you have a lot of fun things to try — better get started now!

How many swingers are there?

As swinging tends to be a surreptitious endeavor, no one really can estimate how many people are involved. Our best guess is at least 5 million, perhaps as many as 10 million, worldwide. The statistic that counts is that there are more playful couples than you could hope to meet in several lifetimes, and their number grows daily.

What sort of people are we likely to meet in swinging?

Just the type you are seeking. (If you give it a fair chance.)

What is the best way to get started?

It may seem less intimidating to get started by correspondence, but, sooner or later, you'll have to face that first personal encounter anyway, so we recommend going directly to a gathering place. There will be less pressure, more options, and you won't waste an evening trying to shake someone who wrote you a bunch of fabrications. There are approximately 300 "public" swing clubs in the United States. If you can't find a club nearby (or you don't care for the one you do find), by all means, try the Internet/magazine approach. Of course, if a friend gave you this booklet, they might well be the key to the door.

How should we choose an Internet contact site?

It's easy enough to find sites that claim to be meeting places for swingers; too easy, in fact, for there are thousands out there. Our best advice, since we certainly haven't tried them all, is to choose the one you are most comfortable with.

You might not be able to judge a book by its cover, but you can get a pretty accurate feel of a site's services by the pictures and ads displayed there. If you're looking for friends, a site full of porno probably isn't a good match. Likewise, avoid sites that aren't honest up front about their requirements and charges. Finally, we suggest that a site that keeps pestering the viewer with additional windows or that is difficult to exit is probably not going to prove as sincere as you might prefer.

Will I be expected to wear a condom?

At clubs that have a very open membership, where people often have sex with folks they've never met before, condoms are commonplace. At the other extreme, at private parties where most everybody knows everybody, condoms are seldom seen. The degree of use varies widely from place to place and time to time. But, you just never can tell. So, even if you believe that latex barriers are the antithesis of intimacy, we advise taking a few along.

Whether male or female, it is a serious breach of etiquette to resist the use of a condom when asked. If you feel the need to discuss the pros and cons, wait until after all sex play is concluded. And, of course, never, ever argue or show anger while at a club or party.

Are most swingers bisexual?

Depends on their gender. The breakdown for females seems to be about 20-40-20-20. That is, 20 percent of women prefer women to men; 40 percent really enjoy sex with women, but prefer men; 20 percent aren't really attracted to, but sometimes will play with, women; and 20 percent find the idea distasteful.

Men are pretty much the other way around. You might never run across a man who prefers sex with men over sex with women. Maybe five percent of men in swinging would admit (under the right circumstances) that they are bisexual, and another 20 to 30 percent are bi-playful. [See page 24.]

Is it a good idea to mix my new swinging friends with my old, non-swinging friends?

Are the swingers really friends? If so, you should certainly be able to trust them not to do anything rude or revealing at your party (or your picnic, graduation, wedding, or any other social event). Just don't expect them to figure out for themselves that everyone in attendance is not a swinger.

Are the non-swingers really friends? If so, you should find it easy to tell them about your new endeavors and they will treat any of your other friends with courtesy.

But, if these folks are simply social acquaintances, then you will need to give the matter more consideration. Using a little common sense, we have had generally good experiences with such mixing.

I have a sensitive job, aren't I putting it at risk by swinging?

In the very few cases we have heard of that someone lost their job because their swinging life was discovered, they had done something pretty dumb (like putting compromising pictures on the Web) that triggered the trouble.

Swingers we have known include doctors, dentists, lawyers, teachers, media personalities, high-ranking military officers and intelligence personnel, and members of several local police departments. Some were more cautious than we, but they all managed to enjoy themselves. For those with sensitive jobs, we recommend sticking to private parties, or at least, avoiding clubs with unrestricted membership.

But, what if I go to a swinging event and I run into someone I know?

This question occurs to just about everyone who entertains ideas of swinging. The common answer is, "Anyone you meet is there too!"

Of course, you've already thought of that. You worry, though, that others might not be as discreet as you or might not have as much to lose from public exposure.

There are two reasons not to be overly concerned. First, people who are indiscreet typically have very short careers in swinging. They don't get invited back to parties and are quickly barred from clubs. Second, if these people tend to talk too much, you probably would have heard them talking already. If you didn't know that they were swingers, they aren't likely to tell anyone that you are.

If you meet someone you know at a club, they might claim that they are "just looking." In which case, you can easily make the same claim. If the encounter occurs at a private party, our best advice is to have a good chuckle and enjoy each other.

How can I be sure I'll like it? Or, at least not hate it? Or, not hate myself for hating it — or for loving it?

You can't be sure that you will enjoy your first (or your fiftieth) swinging experience. But, so what?

No doubt, you have been served terrible food at a restaurant, been disappointed with a novel, suffered through an awful movie, and otherwise not always found life quite as satisfying as you wish. Such experiences did not prevent you from trying other eateries, reading other books, watching more movies, etc. Right?

So, if you don't like your first swinging experience, that's okay. Figure out what went wrong and try again. And, there's no more reason to castigate yourself for a bad experience than there is to feel depressed because you allowed yourself to watch a crappy movie.

On the other hand, if you feel a bit bothered because you liked the experience *too* much, try to remember that all the pleasure you can get is well deserved.

How do I get answers to my other questions?

On the Internet, check out www.theswinginglife.com. This free site has a wealth of information plus links to other important lifestyle sites. In print, we recommend reading *The Lifestyle* by Terry Gould (which covers the historical, cultural, and socio-biological aspects of swinging), and *Together Sex* by yours truly (which is an in-depth "how-to" guidebook for new and experienced swingers). These and others can be purchased through The Swinging Life.

Swing Scene

The Perfect Party

"Honey, I'd like you to imagine that you and I just got home from a swinging party. And you are all excited, and you tell me that was the greatest party you ever attended. You say everything was just perfect and you had the best time of your life. Got all that?"

"Yes dear."

"Okay, so now please close your eyes and describe that party for me in detail."

"Hmmm … Well, to begin with, everybody showed up on time. That did make for a bit of a crowd at the door, but it gave us all a sense of being part of the group as we entered Jim and Sherry's home.

"There was a huge closet in the foyer with plenty of room for our coats so we didn't have to pile them on a bed. Of course, they had several beds stripped down to just the sheets, but we put all of those to better use then holding coats.

"To reduce congestion, Sherry had wisely put the bar in one room and the food in another. That food was not heavy but it was tasty, and it was all in bite-sized portions that were easy to handle. Also, there were bowls of chips, nuts, and other crunchy munchies all around. I always enjoy having a drink so much more when I've got something salty to nibble on."

*"You know, this isn't exactly the response I expected when
I asked you to describe the perfect party. What about
what you did?"*

"I'm getting to that, but the little details make a big differ-
ence in how much everybody enjoys themselves.

"Now, as I was saying, our hosts were just wonderful the
way they introduced the unacquainted guests personally,
mentioning something they were both interested in. You
know, they started a lot of good conversations that way,
instead of just announcing names.

"And it was those conversations that led into the activities
you want to hear about. Those, and the little game that Jim
got going after everyone had a chance to get a drink and
settle in. That was fun and sort of sexy, so it got us all on
the right track.

"Anyway, I was feeling pretty foxy this evening in my little
blue party dress and pretty horny too, since we hadn't had
sex since Tuesday night. This was good because there was
this new couple there and I really liked the guy as soon as
we started talking.

"And I liked the way he couldn't seem to take his eyes off
the tops of my breasts, which, of course, looked really
scrumptious. And I could feel this, like, electricity between
us. So, we're just talking and then, somehow, without plan
or thought, we've moved out of the kitchen and into the
laundry room. Of course, I did catch your eye and you gave
me the nod that means everything's okay."

"Of course you did."

"Right. So, the next thing I know I'm sitting on the washing machine, my panties are off and he's licking me. I'm starting to really goosh, when he straightens up, tells me he's sorry to stop but he really has to have me now, and slides his cock into me in one smooth, loooong, stroke.

"And I haven't even seen it yet! But it feels so very fine, and I cum almost immediately and a moment later I can feel him swelling and spurting inside me.

"So here we are, grinning sheepishly at each other, not quite knowing whether to comment on our "zipless fuck" or just leave it be, when we hear someone call his name. It's his wife. They have trouble with their babysitter and have to leave immediately."

"Not quite the perfect ending I was anticipating."

"Oh, but it made me feel wonderful! When we walked out of the laundry room, he stuffing his half-hard penis back in his pants and I with his cum running down my legs, I was the envy of every gal there. You know that we normally wouldn't do anything so early in the party, but I followed my desire and my intuition and it was a good thing I did or I would have missed out on a really neat time! So I felt rather special.

"Only, I'm still horny, so don't worry, you're going to get yours."

"It's about time."

"Oh, not yet. First you fixed me another drink and we had a snack. The little roast beef sandwiches were delicious with the fresh horseradish sauce — no onions, naturally, we do want to keep ourselves kissable.

"And kiss we did, as we danced a couple of slow dances together. You nuzzling my neck while I whispered my tale of the washing-machine fuck and felt you stiffening against my leg."

> *"To be honest, I wouldn't mind a little leg to stiffen against right now."*

"Hush now. You're the one who got me started on this; so let me finish.

"Well, mid-way through our second dance we sort of bumped into Dan and Laura. You remember them, we partied with them once a couple of years ago and had a great time, but our schedules haven't meshed since. So we started kidding around, and ended up switching partners. Then the music changed to something really wild and the four of us were lost in our own sweaty bump-and-grind session.

"By then I was really getting hot and I stripped off my dress and danced in just my heels and panties."

> *"Must have been pretty sticky panties by then!"*

"I'm ignoring that. ... Then I reached over and pulled up Laura's top — she has such CUTE tits! — and the four of us all started touching and caressing each other, until the music changed again and then we weren't dancing anymore, just rubbing against each other. Fortunately, before our legs gave out, we started moving towards the stairs and went up to a bedroom. I really don't remember anyone suggesting that move, we just sort of went.

"You and Dan sat on the foot of the bed and Laura and I danced for you ... and for each other. Then we came over and started kissing and fondling our respective husbands. Once you and Dan were both good and hard, Laura and I exchanged looks, as if to say 'Look at the goodie I made for you!' and she and I switched places, pushed you two back on the bed, and impaled ourselves on our 'gifts' to each other.

"We rode like that for some time. Laura and I would lean into one another and kiss, then I would kiss Dan, than I would kiss you, then Laura again. I don't recall you and Dan kissing though."

> *"I guess he's just not my type: his tits are okay but I really can't go for the moustache."*

"Hey, you ought to try it, you might like it. Anyway, after awhile we all flipped over with the men on top — my favorite position — we all had fantastic climaxes, then lay for awhile together, just the four of us being cozy."

> *"Thanks hon. That was some party."*

"But, I wasn't finished. I haven't told you about Annie and Bob and the vibrator."

> *"Sorry babe, but we're about out of space and I need you back here in reality."*

"Oh, darling! So you do!" ◀